Table of Contents

Foreword

By Terry Pepper

Co-author of "The Ultimate Guide to West Michigan Lighthouses"

The "black fleet," as the U.S. Lighthouse Service's collection of tenders was known, was a vital component in the operation of every lighthouse district; and nowhere were these vessels more critical than in the two Great Lakes lighthouse districts, where vast distances, rough terrain and winter ice made their mission particularly daunting.

Whether transporting the enormous amounts of materials required to build new lighthouses in remote and dangerous locations, making annual supply runs to every lighthouse in the district, setting hundreds of buoys every spring and retrieving them at the onset of winter, embarking on epic journeys to retrieve the keepers from their posts in weather conditions that would have kept lesser dedicated vessels and their crews in port, or transporting district inspectors, engineers, inspectors and Washington dignitaries on inspection tours, these incredible vessels served as the backbone on which the district's body was built.

Lighthouse tenders were built tough, with reinforced hulls to withstand heavy ice, thick deck planking to support loading of materials and equipment, and equally sturdy lifting booms to facilitate the transfer of bricks, stone, boilers, buoys and untold thousands of tons of coal.

Tender crews were equally tough, working long hours in rough conditions on trips that kept them away from the depot and the comfort of their homes throughout the navigation season. Duty on a lighthouse tender was something to which many aspired, and while named after flowers and shrubs, the crews took great pride in serving on such incongruously named vessels as Marigold, Dahlia and Crocus.

Until now, the critical role played by lighthouse tenders on the Great Lakes has largely remained unheralded. But in this book, Paul Mason sets out to right that wrong, providing the reader with an introduction to virtually all of the tenders that served in the Great Lakes black fleet. In doing so, Paul provides us with a taste of the critical function they served to ensure the safety of mariners throughout the Great Lakes.

Terry Pepper

Introduction

A scene from aboard the USLHT Hyacinth (c.1913). Chief Engineer George J. Lentzner is on the right.

This book is intended to give the recognition due to the U.S. Lighthouse Tender Service that was the backbone of the U.S. Lighthouse Service. While the USLHT Service was nationwide, this book focuses on the ships and crews who were stationed and served on the Great Lakes.

I will open with a brief history of the U.S. Lighthouse Service, and then cover the USLHT Service on the Great Lakes including the history, day-to-day operations and importance of the tenders to the operations of the lighthouses and life-saving stations. I have included stories of the crews' lives, the danger they faced and acts of heroism they performed.

I have included a more detailed history of USLHT Clover from her christening to her decommissioning to give the readers insight into the workings of a tender. Finally, I will include pictures (were available) of every tender that was stationed on the Great Lakes along with the statistics of each ship.

If you love the history of the Great Lakes, and the lighthouse and life-saving stations that were the protectors of all maritime operations – both recreational and commercial – on "The Lakes," you will enjoy learning about the ships and crews that were known as the Lighthouse Tender Service.

Thank you for your interest, and I hope you enjoy the story!

Paul J. Mason

The crew of the Lighthouse Tender USS Sumac removes ice from the deck and stairs using steam hoses hooked to a boiler at Port Richmond, New York (1933)

Chapter 1
History of the U.S. Lighthouse Service

What we know today as the U.S. Lighthouse Service (USLHS) was authorized on August 7, 1789, under the direction of the U.S. Treasury Department. Its authority was to create and maintain various aids to navigation including lighthouses, lightships, buoys, beacons and fog horns. It was also authorized to take control of existing facilities operated by private parties.

By the mid-1800s, there were fifty-five lighthouses along the East Coast and Great Lakes. Private contractors typically handled the building and supply of these facilities, with little or no control by the Lighthouse Service.

In 1838, the Lighthouse Service established eight geographic districts. The challenge of maintaining and supplying the now over two hundred lighthouses and lightships – some in such remote locations they were only accessible by water – was addressed in 1840 with the purchase of the first ship to be used as a lighthouse tender, the former Revenue Cutter Rush.

In 1848, the Lighthouse Service was assigned the additional duty of giving aid and assistance to shipwrecked sailors. This was the forerunner of the U.S. Life-Saving Service.

The Lighthouse Service grew to twelve lighthouse districts by 1852 with the expansion of the United States to the Gulf of Mexico and the Pacific Ocean, and in 1857, the first lighthouse tender contracted specifically for the USLHS was built, USLHT Shubrick.

The USLHS was in disarray during the Civil War, with lighthouses destroyed and tenders sunk or damaged. After the war, the USLHS purchased six former Navy ships for use as lighthouse tenders. These ships were named after flowers, plants and trees, thereby starting this naming tradition for tenders.

During World War I, a number of lighthouse tenders of ocean class served with and under the command of the U.S. Navy. These tenders were returned to the USLHS after the end of the war.

In 1939, the U.S. Lighthouse Service was merged with the U.S. Coast Guard. This involved the transfer of over four thousand personnel, sixty-four lighthouse tenders and almost one thousand, four hundred fifty lighthouses and lightships. Lightships are moored ships that serve as lighthouses, typically used in waters too deep or otherwise unsuitable for lighthouse construction.

Chapter 2
The Lighthouse Tender
Its Origin and Role
In The Lighthouse Service

The Lighthouse Tender was the forerunner of what is known today in the U.S. Coast Guard as a Buoy Tender. The tenders were boats that carried personnel, supplies, materials and repair equipment to and from lighthouses and life-saving stations by water.

They also positioned, removed and serviced aids to navigation such as buoys, range markers and fog horns, and in many instances, rescued sailors shipwrecked at sea. Some lighthouses and life-saving stations were located in such remote areas or on islands and man-made foundations that the only way to get to them was by water. The crews that manned them were totally dependent on the tenders to survive.

The early tenders were sail or steam-powered vessels contracted from private owners for service as lighthouse tenders. These boats were not specifically designed for this purpose, but were adapted to function as best as could be done.

The U.S. Lighthouse Service (USLHS) determined it needed ships that were designed for the unique requirements to efficiently complete their mission, and that they should be owned and under the complete control of the department.

The first ship designed and contracted for building by the USLHS was the USLHT Shubrick, built in 1857. She was a steam-propelled, wood hull, side wheeler.

From that beginning, all future tenders were designed and built for a specific use within the USLHS. Engineering tenders were used for transporting materials and workers to construct aids to navigation such as lighthouses, range lights, fog horn stations and station living quarters.

Supply tenders were used for transporting all the supplies for living at lighthouses and life-saving stations along with the personnel to man them. They also worked the aids to navigation by laying and retrieving buoys and servicing them.

Inspection tenders transported the district inspector on his rounds inspecting all lighthouses and depots. They also functioned as supply tenders. These vessels had special living accommodations on board for the district inspector.

The flag of the U.S. Lighthouse Service

The tenders had unique hull designs that featured curved foredecks, called turtlebacks. This design ensured buoys wouldn't snag on the hull while the tender was alongside servicing them. They also had large working areas forward to store and work the buoys and range markers, and large boom hoists for lifting. Most had prominent storage lockers at the bow called foc'sles *(pronounced fowk-suls)*.

All tenders had black hulls with white superstructure, with their names displayed on the stern in large, brass letters. Brass reliefs of lighthouses were located on the port and starboard sides of the hull at the bow.

The USLHS had a flag designed specifically for this service flown on all tenders.

Chapter 3
The Story of Lighthouse Tenders
on the Great Lakes

The Great Lakes Basin formed approximately 2 billion years ago and the lakes themselves about 15,000 years ago. The five Great Lakes make up the largest group of fresh water lakes in the world, or about 20 percent of all the earth's fresh water.

Modern man has used the lakes (the inland sea) for thousands of years as an easy, inexpensive method to move cargo and people. About 2 million tons of cargo is shipped on the Great Lakes each year at a maximum distance of 2,340 miles from Duluth, Minnesota, to the Gulf of St. Lawrence. With this amount of ship traffic and the perils encountered on the water, it became necessary to construct a network of lighthouses, life-saving stations and aids to navigation to ensure safe passage.

USLHT Dahlia

The first lighthouses were built in 1818 at Buffalo, New York, and Presque Isle, Pennsylvania. These lighthouses, along with many others built later, required servicing to maintain the residents and equipment. The first lighthouse tenders were privately contracted until the U.S. Lighthouse Service (USLHS) purchased two ships to be used on the Great Lakes: the USLHT Lamplighter and Watchful, both wood hull sailing ships of schooner design.

The first steam-powered tender on the lakes was the USLHT Dahlia, put in service in 1874. This vessel continued the USLHS tradition of naming its tenders after flowers, trees and plants. From 1857 to 1939, nineteen lighthouse tenders and three harbor tenders were assigned to Great Lakes duty. You will find photos (when available) along with information on construction, areas of responsibility (home depot) and crew information for each of these vessels in this book.

Tenders were stationed (home port) at USLHS depots located geographically to best serve their areas of responsibility. The crews normally lived in the town closest to the depot while in port. Onboard accommodations served as home during the days or weeks spent underway (sailing).

Their work was dictated by the assignment and included seamanship skills; loading, locating, positioning and servicing, and removal of buoys and other aids to navigation; transporting the district inspector; transporting crews for the lighthouses; transporting construction workers and materials to build and repair lighthouses; ice breaking; search and rescue; and transporting all the necessary supplies to maintain life at the lighthouses.

Most of the lighthouses and life-saving stations on the Great Lakes, especially on northern Lake Huron, Lake Michigan and Lake Superior, were so remote the only way they could be accessed was by water. That made the lighthouse tender the ideal carrier for everything going in or out of those locations.

Supplies meant everything! The lighthouse tenders delivered all the food, cooking oil, lamp oil, heating oil, medical needs, clothing, furniture and everything else necessary for living, including a traveling library. Conversely, the tenders would pick up items that needed repair, empty oil containers, mail and anything else that needed to return to civilization.

I had the privilege of interviewing Bertha Rollo before she passed away in her nineties. Bertha was the granddaughter of Capt. Robert Carlson, who was the lighthouse keeper at Whitefish Point lighthouse from 1903-1931. Bertha lived at the lighthouse with her mother for most of her childhood and young adult life after being brought there when she was two weeks old.

She described to me what an occasion it was when the lighthouse tender arrived on its rounds. The crew members were the only new faces they would see for weeks on end. She said it was like Christmas and her birthday all wrapped up in one celebration. It was a great occasion whenever they were able to restock supplies, get new cloths, hear the news from the "outside world" and just have someone different to talk to.

On the other hand, when the tender was bringing the district inspector for his scheduled inspection of the facilities and personnel, it was a different story. Normally, the keepers knew in advance when the inspector was coming through the grapevine. His visit required a complete and thorough cleaning of everything, and the best formal clothing and uniforms had to be worn. Everything at the lighthouse had to be in good working order.

The Lighthouse District flag

The inspector conducted a white glove inspection, and if anything was amiss, it was entered in the keeper's permanent record of service. The pressure was on before and during the visit.

Bertha described using the tender as a transport for her and her mother to go to the Sault to shop and visit friends, somewhat like how we would use a car, train or airplane today. She had fond memories of the tenders and their crews.

Districts and Depots

The lighthouse tenders were stationed at USLHS depots that were designed and outfitted specifically for tender operations. The depots varied in size, with the largest ones having the most capabilities and specialized workers.

Medium-sized depots featured docking, a few buildings and workers. They mainly housed supplies and some repair equipment. Some depots were nothing more than wharfs, typically unmanned, serving as a place for ships to temporarily leave buoys and other supplies.

The large depots normally housed the district office and had the capability to repair just about anything. They were staffed with blacksmiths and clockworks experts, along with skilled carpenters, masons and any supplies necessary for keeping the tenders operational, along with building and maintaining lighthouses and aids to navigation.

The bigger depots also hosted giant storehouses with every supply item needed to maintain life at the lighthouses and life-saving stations. They were so important that the depot watchmen had their own special service shield (badge).

The Great Lakes were divided geographically into lighthouse districts (LHD), and each district had its own district office/depot. Within each district, additional depots were strategically located to best service the tenders' area of responsibility.

In the early years, the lighthouse districts handling the Great Lakes were the 10th and 11th. As the population of the country expanded westward and more people began living around the Great Lakes, the districts were expanded to the 9th, 10th and 11th.

In 1910, the districts were realigned so the 10th district covered lakes Ontario and Erie; the 11th district included the Detroit River, Lake St. Claire, Lake Huron and the Straits of Mackinac, the St. Marys River, Whitefish Bay and Lake Superior. The 12th district covered Lake Michigan and the bay of Green Bay.

Within the districts were the following depots:

10th – Buffalo, New York (district office); Erie, Pennsylvania; Maumee Bay, Ohio; Rock Island, New York; Sandusky Bay, Ohio.

11th – Detroit, Michigan (district office); Minnesota Point, Minnesota; Sault Ste. Marie, Michigan

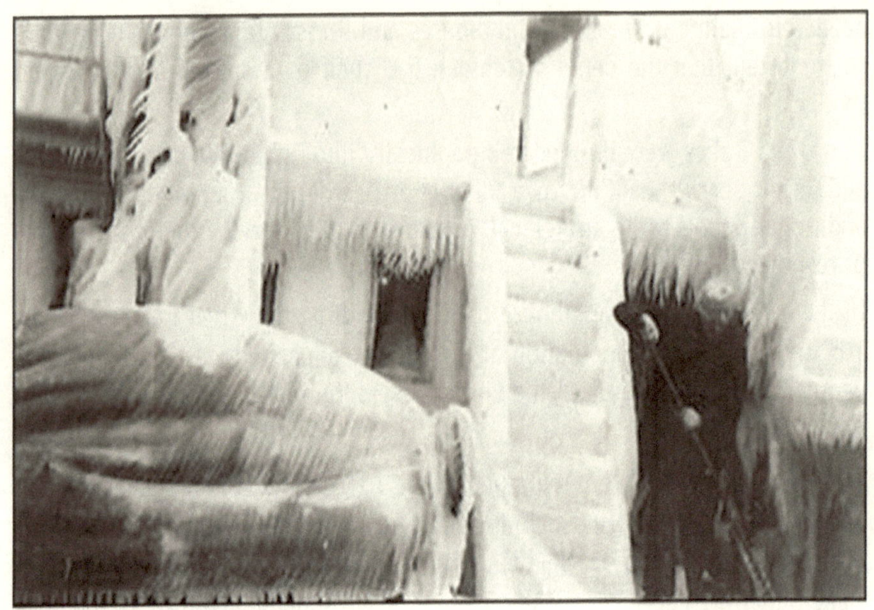

Casey Tylock works to remove ice from the stairs on the forward deck of the USLHT Sumac, 1933.

12th – Milwaukee, Wisconsin (district office); Charlevoix, Michigan; St. Joseph, Michigan

The crew of the lighthouse tender Hyacinth shortly after 1900.

The crews

The Lighthouse Tender Service sought men with seafaring experience to serve on the tenders. All personnel were employees of the U.S. Lighthouse Service. As civil servants, they were required to abide by the rules and regulations set forth by the Lighthouse Board, right down to the specific uniforms required for wear.

The number of crew on a tender depended on the size of the ship. A typical crew included the captain, first, second and third officers, chief engineer and assistant chief engineer, a number of able-bodied seamen, black gang (crew assigned to the engine room) and a cook.

Serving on lighthouse tenders was a very dangerous job for men who primarily were part-time crew. Fatalities and injuries often occurred because of the acetylene gas that was widely used for fuel in lighted buoys and lighthouse beacons. Many crew members also suffered injuries handling buoys, and some experienced frostbite due to exposure working in the elements in the early spring or late fall.

I find no record of a U.S. Lighthouse tender sinking on the Great Lakes; however, there was a sinking of a Canadian tender with the loss of all hands. The Canadian Lighthouse Tender Lambton, a 108-foot, steam-powered, steel hull vessel, left Sault Ste. Marie, Ontario, on the St. Marys River on April 18, 1922, on a mission to take lighthouse crews to their stations on Whitefish Bay and Lake Superior to open the shipping season.

The ill-fated Canadian Lighthouse Tender Lambton

When Canadian officials began receiving calls that the lighthouses were not showing their beacons, they dispatched both Canadian and U.S. search vessels. The U.S. Coast Guard Cutter Cook found debris off the north shore of Lake Superior near Caribou Island and identified the wreckage as being from the Lambton. No survivors were found. There were nineteen lighthouse personnel and three crew members on board when she sank.

Chapter 4
The Story of the USLHT Clover

The U.S. Lighthouse Tender Clover at Whitefish Bay in Lake Superior, c1920. Capt. Nels Larson is on the bridge, with Chief Engineer Richard H. Burdeno standing in the companionway.

The story of the Clover is the story of one boat with two names. The Clover started as a privately owned commercial vessel built at what is known now as the Burger Boat Company in Manitowoc, Wisconsin. The owner named her Two Myrtles after his wife and daughter, who shared the same first name.

The boat was 80 feet long, almost 23 feet wide, and powered by a steam boiler and a single propeller. She was used as a freighter on Lake Michigan, hauling various commodities including hay and fruit. The U.S. Lighthouse Service (USLHS) purchased Two Myrtles in 1907 as a supply vessel to assist in the construction of White Shoals Reef Lighthouse, located about twenty miles west of the current Mackinac Bridge at the northern tip of Lower Michigan.

After this service, Two Myrtles was badly worn and laid up in Milwaukee,

Wisconsin, for two years. In 1913, she went back to Burger Boat and was completely re-worked with the installation of new boilers, engine, her superstructure was completely rebuilt, and a new boom hoist was installed on the forward work deck to facilitate loading and unloading of supplies and aids to navigation (buoys).

Two Myrtles was renamed Clover in the USLHS tradition of naming its tenders after trees, shrubs and flowers. The Clover was assigned to duty in lakes Huron and Superior as a general duty tender and originally ported at Detroit, Michigan, later reported to Sault Ste. Marie, Michigan.

She served a long and distinguished career supplying lighthouses, working aids to navigation, ice breaking, and search and rescue missions in the eastern end of Lake Superior, Whitefish Bay, the St. Marys River and northeastern Lake Huron.

The USLHT Clover was decommissioned in 1934 and turned over to the Federal Emergency Relief Administration. That agency never took possession and later sold the Clover to a private owner, Captain Dan McInnis of DeTour, Michigan, and refitted for use as a commercial freighter.

My grandfather, Richard H. Burdeno, was chief engineer on the Clover for her entire service career. He boarded the then-Two Myrtles in Green Bay, Wisconsin, and stayed with the ship through her refit and thirty-two years of service.

He retired from the Lighthouse Service after Clover's decommissioning with thirty-four years of dedicated service. He passed away in 1944.

Chapter 5
The Great Lakes USLHT Fleet

USLHT Challenge (no photo available)

Service dates: May 1856 to May 1862

Cost : $6,250

Displacement (tons): 120

Dimensions: unknown

Construction/design: wood/supply tender

Power: sail

History: She was purchased from private ownership in May 1856, retaining her original name. Assigned to the 10th Lighthouse District as a supply tender. She was the first lighthouse tender on the Great Lakes. In April 1857, she was renamed USLHT Lamplighter. There were several incidents over the years. In 1857, she was damaged off Isle Royale and repaired in Detroit, Michigan. In 1859, she ran aground off Mackinac Island with minor damage. She was decommissioned in 1862 and sold to a private firm, sailing as a merchant vessel until 1874.

USLHT Dream (no photo available)

Service dates: May 1862 to November 1862

Cost: hired vessel

Displacement (tons): 80

Dimensions: 92 feet

Construction/design: wood/supply tender

Power: sail

History: A hired vessel, she was contracted at $300 per month to replace USLHT Lamplighter, assigned to the 11th Lighthouse District.

USLHT Haze (no photo available)

Service dates: June 1867 to March 1905

Cost: $27,000

Displacement (tons): 328

Dimensions: 137 feet

Construction/design: wood/ supply-engineer

Power: steam/coal fired/single propeller

History: Purchased from a private party (name: Merchant) in June 1867, and assigned to the 12th Lighthouse District. She was the first steam-powered, propeller-driven tender on the Great Lakes. Reassigned to serve both the 10th and 11th lighthouse districts. She had new engines installed in July 1876 and operated out of Detroit (10th district) until March 1905, when she was sold.

USLHT Skylark (Watchful) - no photo available

Service dates: December 1856 to October 1867

Cost: $6,600

Displacement (tons): 146

Dimensions: unknown

Construction/design: wood/supply tender

Power: sail/schooner

History: Privately built in 1854, she was purchased by the Lighthouse Service in 1856 and assigned to the 10th Lighthouse District. She was renamed USLHT Watchful in April 1857, and decommissioned and sold October 1867.

USLHT Lotus (no photo available)

Service dates: 1880 to 1901

Cost: $5,000

Displacement (tons): 15

Dimensions: 40 feet

Construction/design: wood/harbor tender

Power: steam-fired coal/single propeller

Crew: unknown

History: USLHT Lotus was a harbor tender serving in the 11th Lighthouse District. Decommissioned and sold in 1901.

USLHT Warrington

Service dates: 1870 to 1910

Cost: $25,000

Displacement (tons): 410

Dimensions: 260 feet

Construction/design: wood/ supply-construction

Power: steam fired/single propeller

Crew: 5 officers, 15-19 crew

History: Purchased from a private party in 1868, she was refitted and commissioned in 1870 and assigned to the 11th Lighthouse District as a supply/construction tender. She had a fire onboard in 1879 and incurred $16,000 in damage. Working out of Detroit, Michigan, she participated in the construction of the Spectacle Reef Lighthouse (upper Lake Huron). In 1898, she was transferred to the 10th Lighthouse District out of Buffalo, NEW YORK, and assigned as an engineering tender. She was sold to a private party in 1910 and ran aground in 1911, declared a total loss.

USLHT Dahlia

Service dates: 1874 to 1909

Cost: $81,800

Displacement (tons): 426

Dimensions: 141 feet

Construction/design: iron/inspection tender

Power: steam fired/single propeller

Crew: 6 officers, 15 crew

History: Dahlia was the first tender specifically contracted and built to serve on the Great Lakes, and was the first to carry a botanical name. She was assigned to the 11th Lighthouse District as an inspector tender. Later, she was reassigned to the 9th Lighthouse District. She was sold to a private party in 1909, serving as a passenger boat (Flor M Hill) on Lake Michigan and sank in Chicago, Illinois, in 1912, crushed by ice.

USLHT Marigold

Service dates: October 1891 to December 1945

Cost: $85,000

Displacement (tons): 587

Dimensions: 159 feet

Construction /design: iron/inspection tender

Power: steam-fired coal/single propeller

Crew: 2-6 officers, 19-24 crew

History: Built as an inspection tender and assigned to the 11th Lighthouse District for her entire service. She served aids to navigation in lakes Superior and Huron. Part of the transfer to the U.S. Coast Guard in 1939, she was the oldest active tender (WAGL-235). When decommissioned in 1945, she had served over 54 years. Sold to a private party in 1946, she was converted to a dredge working out of Bay City, Michigan, until 1980.

USLHT Amaranth in 1892 (National Archives)

USLHT Amaranth

Service dates: April 1892 to September 1945

Cost: $75,000

Displacement (tons): 1053

Dimensions: 166 feet

Construction/design: steel/engineering tender

Power: steam coal-fired/single propeller

Crew: 5-6 officers, 17-24 crew

History: Commissioned as an engineering tender, she was assigned to the 11th Lighthouse District. She serviced lighthouses and aids to navigation on Lake Superior. She had a heroic occurrence in October 1901, participating in the rescue of a lake freighter off Copper Harbor, Michigan. Reclassified a bay/sound tender in July 1920, she was damaged while servicing Passage Island Lighthouse and subsequently repaired and restored to service. She was also part of the transfer of assets to the U.S. Coast Guard (WAGL-201). She was the second-oldest tender in service. Assigned to Duluth, Minnesota, she was decommissioned and sold to a private party in 1946. She served as a lake freighter (South Wind) until 1954.

USLHT Sumac

Service dates: June 1903 to July 1937

Cost: $115,000

Displacement (tons): 875

Dimensions: 168 feet

Construction/design: steel/inspection tender

Power: steam coal-fired/single propeller

Crew: 5-6 officers, 18-23 crew

History: An inspection tender assigned to the 9th Lighthouse District, Milwaukee, Wisconsin, she was later re-designated a bay/sound tender in 1925 and assigned to the 12th Lighthouse District. She was decommissioned and sold to a private owner in 1937, and became a tug (Oscar Lebtinen) towing log rafts until 1957.

USLHT Hyacinth passes a Coast Guard station as she leaves
Two Rivers, Wisconsin, harbor.

USLHT Hyacinth

Service dates: June 1903 to November 1945

Cost: $115,000

Displacement (tons): 950

Dimensions: 160 feet

Construction/design: steel/ engineering tender

Power: steam coal-fired/single propeller

Crew: 5-6 officers, 18-20 crew

History: Assigned to the 9th Lighthouse District, Milwaukee, Wisconsin, as an engineering tender, she served her entire career on Lake Michigan.

The USLHT Crocus in front

USLHT Crocus

Service dates: July 1905 to July 1946

Cost: $ 120,000

Displacement (tons): 1,035

Dimensions: 125 feet

Construction/design: steel/inspector tender

Power: steam coal-fired/single propeller

Crew: 5-6 officers, 20-23 crew

History: An inspection tender assigned to the 10th Lighthouse District, Buffalo, New York, in 1932, her power plant was upgraded to oil fired and re-assigned to Detroit, Michigan. She was transferred to the U.S. Coast Guard (WAGL-210) and was stationed in Toledo, Ohio.

USLHT Aspen

Service dates: May 1906 to January 1947

Cost: $70,500

Displacement (tons): 415

Dimensions: 125 feet

Construction/design: steel/bay/sound tender

Power: steam coal-fired/single propeller

Crew: 4 officers, 8-14 crew

History: Built as a bay/sound tender, she was assigned to the 11th Lighthouse District, Detroit, Michigan. She had a new upgrade boiler installed in 1932 and was transferred to the U.S. Coast Guard (WAGL-204). She was home-ported in Sault Ste. Marie, Michigan, and subsequently sold to a private owner in 1948.

USLHT Two Myrtles as she looked in 1909

USLHT Two Myrtles (USLHT Clover)

Service dates: 1908 to 1935

Cost: $5,700

Displacement (tons): 205

Dimensions: 88 feet

Construction/design: wood/engineering tender

Power: steam coal-fired/single propeller

Crew: 2-4 officers, 5-8 crew

History: Two Myrtles, named after the original owner's wife and daughter, was purchased by the lighthouse service in 1908. Retaining her original name, she was commissioned USLHT Two Myrtles and assigned to the 11th Lighthouse District, Milwaukee, Wisconsin, as an engineering tender. She was re-worked in 1911 and re-named the USLHT Clover in 1912, serving in Detroit and Sault Ste. Marie, Michigan. She was rebuilt again in 1932 and lengthened from 88 feet to 93 feet. Decommissioned and sold in 1935, she was used as a lake freighter and returned to her original name (SS Two

Myrtles), finally abandoned in 1947.

USLHT Sundew (no photo available)

Service dates: 1922 to 1939

Cost: $115,800

Displacement (tons): 710

Dimensions: 101 feet

Construction/design: wood/unknown

Power: steam coal-fired/single propeller

Crew: 2 officers, 8 crew

History: Originally a U.S. Navy mine sweeper, the U.S. Lighthouse Service took possession in 1922 at no cost to the service. She was originally assigned to Key West, Florida, and later transferred to the 10th Lighthouse District on Lake Ontario.

USLHT Cherry

Service dates: 1932 to 1964

Cost: $109,000

Displacement (tons): 254

Dimensions: 86 feet

Construction/design: steel/bay/sound tender

Power: diesel/single propeller

Crew: 2 officers, 5-10 crew

History: Assigned originally to the 10th Lighthouse District, Buffalo, New York, she was transferred to the U.S. Coast Guard and reassigned to Sault Ste. Marie, Michigan, as a buoy tender. In 1965, she was transferred to the government of the Republic of Surinam in South America.

USLHT Tamarack

Service dates: 1934 to 1970

Cost: $234,000

Displacement (tons): 400

Dimensions: 124 feet

Construction/design: steel/bay/sound tender

Power: diesel/single propeller

Crew: 4 officers, 10 crew

History: First assigned to the 11th Lighthouse District, she was transferred to the 9th U.S. Coast Guard District, stationed in Manitowoc, Wisconsin, and later reassigned to Sault Ste. Marie, Michigan. She was decommissioned in 1970 and sold in 1971.

USLHT Hollyhock

Service dates: 1937 to 1982

Cost: $347,000

Displacement (tons): 885

Dimensions: 174 feet

Construction/design: steel/coastal tender

Power: steam/twin propellers

Crew: 4 officers, 69 crew

History: Assigned to the 12th Lighthouse District, Milwaukee, Wisconsin, she was transferred to the U.S. Coast Guard (WEAGL-220) and converted to diesel power. She served in Detroit, Michigan, before being decommissioned in 1982 and sold to a private owner (Good News mission ship). She ended up sunk as an artificial reef off Florida.

USLHT Dahlia (second version) - no photo available

Service dates: 1933 to 1964

Cost: $69,000

Displacement (tons): 160

Dimensions: 81 feet

Construction/design: steel/bay/sound tender

Power: diesel/single propeller

Crew: 3 officers, 4-10 crew

History: Named after the original built in 1874, the Dahlia was assigned to the 11th Lighthouse District, Detroit, Michigan. She was decommissioned and transferred to the government of the Republic of Surinam in South America in 1965.

The USCGC Walnut near Belle Isle in the Detroit River, December 12, 1939

USLHT Walnut

Service dates: 1939 to 1982

Cost: $389,000

Displacement (tons): 885

Dimensions: 174 feet

Construction/design: steel/coastal tender

Power: steam/twin propellers

Crew: 4 officers, 69 crew

History: Walnut was the same class cutter as Hollyhock (above). She was assigned to the 11th Lighthouse District, Cleveland, Ohio, servicing aids to navigation in lakes Huron and Superior. She was transferred to the U.S. Coast Guard and decommissioned in 1982 before being transferred to the government of Honduras.

USLHT Maple

Service dates: 1939 to 1973

Cost: $190,000

Displacement (tons): 342

Dimensions: 122 feet

Construction/design: steel/bay/sound tender

Power: 2 diesels/twin propellers

Crew: 1 officer, 27 crew

History: Assigned to the 10th Lighthouse District and transferred to the U.S. Coast Guard (WAGL-234), she was later decommissioned in 1973 and transferred to the U.S. Navy and eventually to the Environmental Protection Agency (Roger R. Simmons). She was home-ported in Milwaukee, Wisconsin, monitoring water pollution on the Great Lakes. She later moored at St. Ignace, Michigan, as a maritime museum before being sold in 2008 to a marina in Milwaukee, where she was refitted for use in giving cruises of the harbor and lakeshore area. As of 2009, she had been repainted red and was boarded up in the Kinnickinnick River in Milwaukee (bottom photo).

Conclusion

I hope this book has given you a new perspective on the operations of the U.S. Lighthouse Service and enlightened you about a little-known branch of that service.

I have attempted to include all the tenders that, through my research, served on the Great Lakes. If I missed any, I apologize.

There were over ninety tenders over the history of the Lighthouse Service, not counting the many smaller work boats, lightships and other support units.

I've only covered the service on the Great Lakes here. There are a few books out there that do a wonderful job of documenting the lighthouse tenders throughout the United States. One of those books is *"United States Lighthouse Service Tenders 1840-1939,"* authored by Douglas Peterson. Terry Pepper's website is another great source for information on tenders at

http://terrypepper.com

I thank you for taking the time to read this book!

Paul J. Mason

Acknowledgements

I want to thank the following people and organizations who, without their help, guidance and encouragement, I never would have had the ability or drive to complete this book.

Bonnie Groessl and Mike Dauplaise, of M&B Global Solutions Inc., who through their little notice in the local newspaper about a free seminar for fledgling authors, showed me a pathway to publication and then took me step by step through the process. Thanks for all your patience in working with an old, low- to none-tech guy.

Michael Strohschein, my son-in-law, who took his father-in-law through all those computer pitfalls and got the ideas in my head converted to new world technology. Thanks for putting up with the "old guy"!

Jamie Strohschien, my daughter and Michael's wife, for "loaning" Michael out to assist me.

Terry Pepper, the "guru of Great Lakes lighthouse history," for allowing me to bug him when I was stuck on facts and being gracious enough to take time out of his very busy schedule to authenticate my book with his foreword.

Douglas Peterson, author of "United States Lighthouse Service Tenders," for his wonderful book and the first in-depth recognition of the lighthouse tenders and their extreme importance to the success of the U.S. Lighthouse Service.

Wisconsin Maritime Museum in Manitowoc, Wisconsin, for allowing me to visit their Great Lakes archives library and purchase the wonderful photographs relating to the day-to-day life of the crews of the lighthouse tenders.

Patrick Hornberger, president of Eastwind Publishing, and Bruce Lynn, executive director of Great Lakes Shipwreck Historical Society, for allowing us to use pictures and facts from their publications.

Thank you!

Paul J. Mason

Glossary

Acetylene gas – A highly flammable gas used for illuminating lighthouse lamps and lighted buoys

Bow – The front end of a boat

Buoy – An anchored floating maritime marker usually indicating a channel or regulated waterway

Boom hoist – A derrick-type structure designed for loading and unloading heavy items on and off the deck of a boat

Depot – (As in USLHS depot) A fixed location on land with buildings and docks; used for storage and repair

Displacement – The calculated tonnage weight of a boat based on the amount of water it displaces

District inspector – A Lighthouse Service supervisor responsible for the operations of lighthouses

Foc'sle – A prominent high structure at the bow of a boat used for storage

Fog horn – An audible signal used to warn boats of dangerous areas in limited viability

Homeport – A base docking location for a tender, usually a district or satellite depot

Hull – The base structure of a boat

LHD – The designation for lighthouse district; a geographic area as part of the United States

Port side – The left side of a boat facing the bow

Range marker – A fixed maritime aid to navigation used to align a course into a harbor entrance

Schooner – A type of sailing ship with sails configured fore and aft

Starboard side – The right side of a boat facing the bow

Stern – The back end of a boat

Superstructure – The area built on the hull of a boat usually containing the wheelhouse, cabins, crew's quarters, galley and storage

Tender – A boat designed and used by the USLHS to service lighthouses, aids to navigation, carry cargo and construction materials, along with transporting personnel

USLHS – The designation for United States Lighthouse Service

USLHT – The designation for United States Lighthouse Tender

Photo Credits

In order of appearance:

- Author's personal collection, purchased from the Wisconsin Maritime Museum

- Author's personal collection, purchased from the Wisconsin Maritime Museum

- Author's personal collection, purchased from Wisconsin Maritime Museum

- Lighthouse Digest

- Terry Pepper collection

- Lighthouse Digest

- Lighthouse Digest

- Lighthouse Digest

- Author's personal collection, purchased from the Wisconsin Maritime Museum

- Author's personal collection, purchased from the Wisconsin Maritime Museum

- Great Lakes Historical Shipwreck Museum

- Author's personal collection, from Valley Camp Ship Museum

- Terry Pepper collection

- Terry Pepper collection

- Terry Pepper collection

- Author's personal collection, purchased from the Wisconsin Maritime Museum

- Author's personal collection, purchased from the Wisconsin Maritime Museum

- Author's personal collection, purchased from the Wisconsin Maritime Museum

- Douglas Peterson, United States Lighthouse Service Tenders

- Author's personal collection, purchased from the Wisconsin Maritime Museum

- Author's personal collection, purchased from the Wisconsin Maritime

Museum

- Douglas Peterson, United States Lighthouse Service Tenders

- Author's personal collection, purchased from the Wisconsin Maritime Museum

- Douglas Peterson, United States Lighthouse Service Tenders

- Douglas Peterson, United States Lighthouse Service Tenders

- Douglas Peterson, United States Lighthouse Service Tenders

- Terry Pepper collection